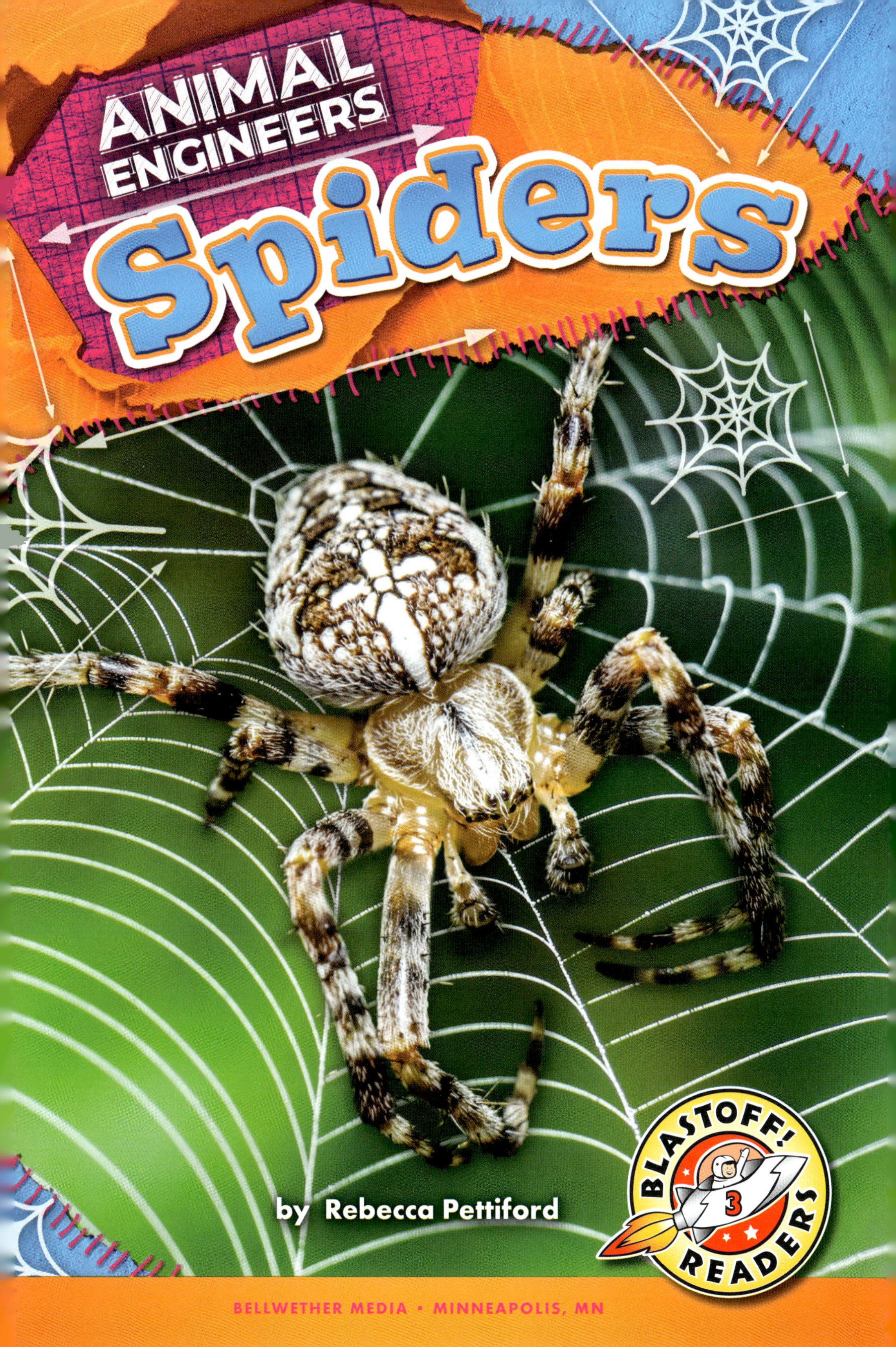
ANIMAL ENGINEERS
Spiders
by Rebecca Pettiford
BLASTOFF! READERS
3
BELLWETHER MEDIA • MINNEAPOLIS, MN

Blastoff! Readers are carefully developed by literacy experts to build reading stamina and move students toward fluency by combining standards-based content with developmentally appropriate text.

Level 1 provides the most support through repetition of high-frequency words, light text, predictable sentence patterns, and strong visual support.

Level 2 offers early readers a bit more challenge through varied sentences, increased text load, and text-supportive special features.

Level 3 advances early-fluent readers toward fluency through increased text load, less reliance on photos, advancing concepts, longer sentences, and more complex special features.

★ **Blastoff! Universe**

Reading Level

Grade K

Grades 1–3

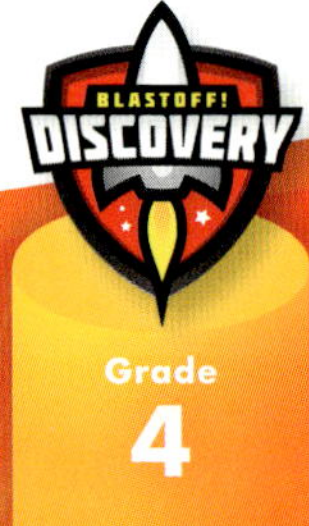

Grade 4

This edition first published in 2025 by Bellwether Media, Inc.

Library of Congress Cataloging-in-Publication Data

LC record for Spiders available at: https://lccn.loc.gov/2024015048

Editor: Rachael Barnes Designer: Josh Brink

Printed in the United States of America, North Mankato, MN.

Table of Contents

Building with Silk 4
Planning a Web 8
Time to Build! 12
The Web Is Ready! 18
Glossary 22
To Learn More 23
Index 24

Building with Silk

Spiders are **arachnids**. They spin thin threads of **silk**. Some spiders use silk to line their **burrows**.

Silk is also a powerful hunting tool. Many spiders use silk to build sticky webs that trap **prey**.

burrow

Spiders live on nearly all land on Earth. Some live in buildings! Their **habitats** include mountains, **wetlands**, forests, and **deserts**.

Spider Range Map

range =

There are over 50,000 **species**. Different species use silk in different ways. Most build webs.

Planning a Web

ballooning

Spiders **disperse** shortly after they **hatch**. Many spiders do this by ballooning. They climb up high. They raise their **abdomens** and release silk from their **spinnerets**.

The silk catches the wind and carries the spiders away.

Building Tools

spinnerets

legs

When spiders reach their new homes, many build webs. They choose spots that are in the path of their prey.

orb web

Building Materials

silk

plants

walls

rocks

Some spiders build webs near the ground. Others build on plants or rocks. Many build orb webs.

Time to Build!

Orb webs start with the first point of a **bridge thread**. Some spiders walk the thread to its second point. Others let wind push the thread.

Spiders walk across their bridge, adding more silk. The bridge gets stronger.

bridge
thread

Spiders make a loose thread beneath the bridge. They connect another thread to a third point to form a Y.

Spiders add strong **radial threads**. They are built out from the center of the Y.

Next, spiders make **spirals**. The first spiral is made with dry thread. The last spiral is strong and sticky to catch prey.

prey

When their webs trap prey, spiders feel movement on the threads!

The Web Is Ready!

Wind, rain, and animals can destroy spider webs. Some spiders fix their webs. Other spiders eat them to replace their silk supply.

Orb web builders often spin new webs every day.

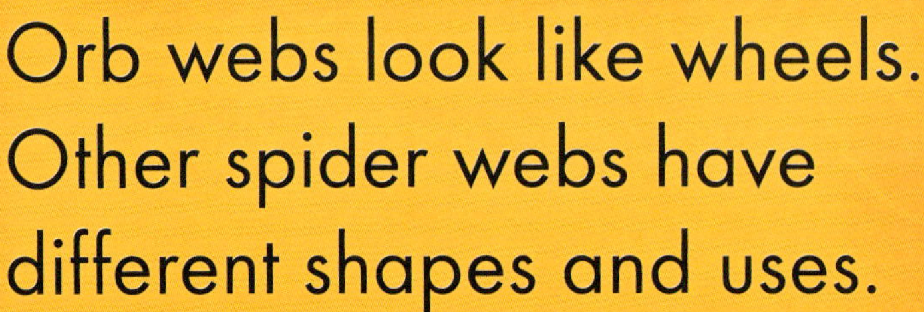

Orb webs look like wheels. Other spider webs have different shapes and uses.

In any shape, spider silk is one of the strongest building tools in the world!

Types of Spider Webs

- these are some of the most common spider webs
- each of these webs helps spiders find and catch prey in different ways

Glossary

abdomens—the back parts of the bodies of arachnids

arachnids—animals with two body segments and four pairs of legs

bridge thread—a silk thread that connects two points to begin an orb web

burrows—holes or tunnels in the ground that some animals use for homes

deserts—areas of land that get little rain

disperse—to spread out

habitats—the natural homes of plants and animals

hatch—to break out of an egg

prey—animals that are hunted by other animals for food

radial threads—strong silk threads that come out from the center point of orb webs

silk—a thin and strong thread made by spiders

species—kinds of animals

spinnerets—the silk-spinning body parts of spiders

spirals—shapes made by circling around a center point

wetlands—areas of land that are covered with low levels of water for most of the year

To Learn More

AT THE LIBRARY

Becker, Trudy. *Tarantulas*. Lake Elmo, Minn.: Focus Readers, 2023.

Mattern, Joanne. *What's So Scary About Spiders?* South Egremont, Mass.: Red Chair Press, 2023.

Nicholas, Christopher. *Spiders*. London, U.K.: Sequoia Kids Media, 2023.

ON THE WEB

FACTSURFER

Factsurfer.com gives you a safe, fun way to find more information.

1. Go to www.factsurfer.com.
2. Enter "spiders" into the search box and click 🔍.
3. Select your book cover to see a list of related content.

Index

abdomens, 8
arachnids, 4
ballooning, 8
bridge thread, 12, 13, 14
building materials, 11
building tools, 9, 20
burrows, 4, 5
disperse, 8
ground, 11
habitats, 6
hatch, 8
orb webs, 10, 11, 12, 19, 20
plants, 11
prey, 4, 10, 16, 17
radial threads, 15
range, 6, 7
rocks, 11
shapes, 20, 21
silk, 4, 7, 8, 9, 12, 18, 20
species, 7
spinnerets, 8
spirals, 16
threads, 4, 12, 13, 14, 15, 16, 17
types of spider webs, 21
webs, 4, 7, 10, 11, 12, 17, 18, 19, 20
wind, 9, 12, 18

The images in this book are reproduced through the courtesy of: MarcinWojc, cover (hero spider); lovelyday12, cover / back cover (background web); nico99, p. 3; samray, p. 4 (silk web); Macronatura.es, pp. 4-5; Ranahpixel, pp. 6-7; Michael Hutchinson/ Alamy, pp. 8-9; Kurt Hohenbichler, p. 9 (spinnerets); Chase D'animulls, p. 9 (spider); DMITRII STARTCEV, pp. 10-11; Ian Fletcher, pp. 11 (silk), 20; Kristine Rad, p. 11 (plants); RelentlessImages, p. 11 (walls); Andreas Muth-Hegener, p. 11 (rocks); kojihirano, p. 12; Sergey Zuenok, pp. 12-13; Philip Marsh/ Alamy, pp. 14-15; Richard Bedford/ Alamy, p. 15; Eugene Kalenkovich, pp. 16-17; LionH/ Getty, p. 17; GeG/ Alamy, pp. 18-19; Sinelev, p. 19; magnetix, pp. 20-21 (web); Donna Bollenbach, p. 21 (orb web); IJPhoto, p. 21 (tunnel web); kzww, p. 21 (tangle web); Wakhron, p. 21 (sheet web); ervin herman, p. 23.